Cultural Sensitivity
For
Crazy Rich Asians

The Secret to Success

- Paul F. Davis -

The film "Crazy Rich Asians" has caught a lot of controversy from the Asian community for its oversight of the entire Asian populace, socioeconomics of the region, and the casting of the actors in the film who tend to be predominately only one ethnicity (mostly Chinese).

Nevertheless the film has its merits in that it helps Asians feel proud about an all Asian cast, regardless if the majority are only from one ethnicity and fail to adequately and fully represent Singapore where the film supposedly was made.

Singapore is a nation with a beautiful mix of Chinese, Malay and Indian people (a lovely diaspora that peacefully coexists, interacts and collaborates daily to achieve great things in a nation ranked among the best in the world for ease of doing business). Ye the film "Crazy Rich Asians" shows a predominately Chinese cast and brown Asians like Malays and Indian are nowhere to be seen in the movie.

Interestingly, the word *diaspora* itself has evolved as much as the ethnic groups it seeks to define that have migrated and scattered worldwide. Among the definitions for the word diaspora are: the spread or dissemination of something (be it language or culture) originally confined to a local, homogenous group. This definition of diaspora accounts for the spread of American culture worldwide via its movies and music. The British effectively colonized the world and succeeded at spreading their language throughout the earth, it now being the language of international business, commerce and trade worldwide.

The word diaspora also applies to any group that has been dispersed outside its traditional homeland, including involuntarily (as in African and Indian slaves that were taken to the Americas and Caribbean among other places). Oppressed religious groups (another diaspora) in Europe historically traveled to the "new world" in America (predominately the United States and Canada) to escape harsh conditions and pursue religious freedom of expression. Thus the many definitions for the word diaspora reveal minority peoples living among the prevailing majority in any given country and culture are too vitally important and to be included when defining a nation, region, or continent of people.

The word *diaspora* originated to describe the scattered Jewish people throughout countries beyond Israel after Babylonian invasion and captivity. Thus people groups often migrate as a survival mechanism to escape oppression and harsh conditions (be they economic or otherwise) in their nation of origin. Nowadays people also migrate, as one taxi driver in New York City once told me, seeking "greener pastures" (for cash and financial opportunities that they perceive do not exist in their homeland). Today the global economy is such, people can live and work nearly anywhere (and even virtually online to permit them to live anywhere they choose assuming the governmental laws in their nation of choice are welcoming).

Displaced peoples throughout the earth also occurs due to natural disasters: typhoons, floods, drought (lack of water), disease, pestilence, wars, along with racial and religious discrimination (all of which make conditions too harsh to stay and remain in the present situation and place). People in wealthy and comfortable countries would do well to remember this when foreigners show up and immigrate to their nations. In other words, we who are well off should welcome strangers with kindness, because quite possibly this could be us one day. We never should assume conditions beyond our control will always remain the same and be favorable for us. Sometimes adaptation and migration is necessary as a means of survival and to improve the quality of life for yourself and your family. Therefore those who migrate abroad should be respected for their intelligence, bravery, courage and resourcefulness (rather than demonized for leaving all and suffering great hardship en route to a new country). Just because people do not look, talk, dress, behave and believe like us does not decrease their value in the eyes of God as a human being. We are all human beings in God's loving family here on earth and to survive we all need to learn to be more kind, peaceful and welcoming of others. It is a known and proven fact that people who are inclusive, kind and collaborate tend to do better socially (having meaningful relationships and social connections), physically (meaning they live longer), and financially. None of us are as strong as all of us. Therefore when we come together and combine our collective strengths (as schools, temples, mosques, churches - educational and faith based communities do daily and weekly throughout Asia and the earth) we can accomplish so much more, have so much more fun along the way, discover our purpose on earth, and learn to love others and happily and harmoniously live together.

Today the word *diaspora* has even morphed into attempts to define and describe the spread of various aspects of cultures and subcultures (musically, related to style and fashion, political ideologies related to preferred forms of government, and schools of religious thought). Certainly it is evident throughout the world that African American rap and hip-hop music has impacted the thinking and culture of millions of youth worldwide. To evidence this assertion, you can watch a Chinese rap band perform "Made In China" for a good laugh and eye-opening video that shows Chinese young men "singing," boldly self-actualizing and stating how they see themselves and life, and striving to live large and in charge like famous rappers reaping

fame and fortunes in America.

https://www.youtube.com/watch?v=rILKm-DC06A&index=1&list=RDrILKm-DC06A

Asia is a massive, magnificent and dynamic

continent where two-thirds of the world's

population in total live and thrive. Thus the

contention over the film "Crazy Rich Asians" that

forgot about all of the other people and nations

within Asia. Allow me to name a few of the many

Asian groups of people in the continent overlooked

by the film who are also among the most ten

populated nations on earth: Indians (who account

for the world's most populated nation in Asia and

world's largest democracy, a concept of government

perhaps foreign to most Chinese, certainly

experientially as many Chinese activists are

pursuing and protesting for democracy in places

like Hong Kong and elsewhere), Indonesians (also located in Asia comprising the fourth most populated nation on earth, the nation with the fastest growing number of millionaires in the continent and the nation with the most Muslims worldwide), Pakistanis (the sixth most populated nation on earth also in Asia and the former home to terrorist Osama Bin Laden), Bangladeshis (the eighth most populated nation on earth located in Asia originating from the historical region of Bengal and a nation where many of the world's textiles and clothing is made), and Japan (the tenth most populated nation on earth, one where 9 of the 10 top chefs in the world would like to live, and a civilized nation with the lowest infant mortality on earth and some of the longest living people before McDonalds and "American" fast food arrived).

Allow me to list all of the nations located in Asia for those of us who have forgotten, never imagined or conceived of the idea (thinking only of themselves locally as we all can tend to do as we grind on daily trying to survive and provide for ourselves), or failed to grasp the enormity of the continent and its many magnificent and wonderful people. For whatever reason the region of Asia historically has been geographically defined to include Central Asia, Western Asia (or Southwestern Asia, or the Middle East minus Egypt). Asians themselves can decide whether or not they want to include the Middle East in their definition (just like some African Americans don't consider all black people to be "black" as they have the color, but don't feel all blacks are their cultural kind). I will alphabetize the Asian nations when listing them below with no favoritism or priority being given otherwise.

1. Afghanistan

2. Armenia

3. Azerbaijan

4. Bahrain

5. Bangladesh

6. Bhutan

7. Brunei

8. Cambodia

9. China

10. Georgia

11. Hong Kong

12. India

13. Indonesia

14. Iran

15. Iraq

16. Israel

17. Japan

18. Jordan

19. Kazakhstan

20. South Korea

21. North Korea

22. Kuwait

23. Kyrgyzstan

24. Laos

25. Lebanon

26. Macau

27. Malaysia

28. Maldives

29. Mongolia

30. Myanmar

31. Nepal

32. Oman

33. Pakistan

34. Philippines

35. Qatar

36. Saudi Arabia

37. Singapore

38. Sri Lanka

39. Syria

40. Tajikistan

41. Taiwan

42. Thailand

43. Timor Leste

44. Turkey

45. Turkmenistan

46. United Arab Emirates

47. Uzbekistan

48. Vietnam

49. Yemen

As for me, I am someone who has lived and traveled throughout Asia (as well as to 89 nations worldwide). I have lived in Asia for 6 years within the following countries and territories: Taiwan, Hong Kong, China, India, Indonesia, Malaysia, Thailand, Myanmar and Vietnam. I also have written books about China and Vietnam (particularly environmental health, water and food security). I therefore am intimately acquainted with Asians and have often corrected Americans in the United States who failed to discern the difference of various Asian ethnicities and groups (among whom are Sikhs from India and Singapore, who are often mistaken for being Muslims because of the large turban atop their heads). Moreover I sometimes jokingly refer to myself as an "egg" or "an Asian man trapped in a white man's body." I also negotiate tough like a Chinese when doing business whenever I can, but also exercise restraint to cultivate and build long-term relationships in the process as do many wise, culturally and business savvy Asians.

Asian Americans are presently (and rightfully) suing Harvard University for fostering diversity as a means to diversify their student body at the exclusion of qualified Asian Americans (and outstanding students from many other ethnicities including Caucasians and the majority of high school class valedictorians who apply for admissions). The United States Department of Justice is conducting a full-fledged investigation into Harvard and other elite American universities admissions criteria and selection process.

Asian Americans are rightfully protesting and vocalizing they too have a dream and don't want to take the backseat because of diversity quotas at top universities. Elsewhere in Asia, Hong Kong taxpayers just paid for the longest sea bridge to be constructed by China (connecting Hong Kong, Macau and Zuhai). Although most bridges are known for transcending barriers and bringing people together, China's new landmark bridge will only allow elite passengers who pay and are approved by the government to travel across it (meaning the majority of Hong Kong taxpayers who bore the financial burden to build the bridge will never get to use it). This again is an unfair practice occurring in Asia that discriminates against hardworking citizens and taxpayers who deserve equal access and far better treatment.

Governments throughout the world are preventing equal access to information and quieting the voices of Asians through censorship, often in the name of monitoring and removing "fake news" that does not align with the prevailing "leaders" in government's ideology and vision for the future.

Mainland China censors the Internet, blocking and restricting the following websites (among others): Google, Facebook, YouTube and Bloomberg (among other news sources that may report anything unfavorable about Beijing, China, and/or President Xi). Thus many Chinese in the mainland are uninformed, misinformed and subject to years of ongoing government propaganda. Thus their oversight and lack of knowledge, along with their cultural conditioning, is not entirely their fault (as they are subject to the environment in which they were born, raised, educated and brought up). Therefore vocal opposition of things Asian, Chinese and Beijing may never reach the ears of many Chinese who desperately need truth to enlighten them. Nevertheless we with free access to the Internet and the international community, must continue to lift up our voices and sound the alarm, to increase the likelihood of truth entering and piercing the bamboo curtain and reaching those in need of illumination and revelation.

Upon learning of the controversy related to the film "Crazy Rich Asians" I put together an assignment for my 9th grade students (Thai and Taiwanese) in Thailand to encourage them to think about the importance of the film and the surrounding cultural issues.

Since the film had no Thai, Indian, or Malay actors in it; perhaps calling it "Asians" was an exaggeration, presumptuous and a stretch (since the primary focus was on Chinese). Yet the book and film likely reached and sold more people by choosing to use "Asians" rather than Chinese in the title. Thus some economic motivations likely came into play when the title for the novel and film were made (like much of what China does as a nation - for example when artificially manipulating and devaluing its currency to stimulate export of products and sales worldwide). Yet it is always vitally important to distinguish between a nation and its government versus the true citizenry and people of a given nation. Undoubtedly, the two are often vastly different and neither can fully represent the other (although the politicians of the governments of the world often try to).

Prudent and thoughtful questions are the door and gateway to wisdom. As the Chinese proverb states: "When the student is ready, the teacher appears." Thus insightful questions and eliciting information from one's teachers and mentors shows intellectual curiosity on the part of the student and a readiness to learn.

Thus rather than tell my Asian students HOW to think and giving them the answers, instead I prefer to ask insightful questions and let them reflect, search their hearts, probe and examine their own life experiences, conduct research online and elsewhere, and thereafter come up with their own internal truth and answers to direct their lives forward (considering each of us have different relational and professional paths and pursuits).

It is hard to gain insight without humbling yourself and asking questions. None of us know everything and all of us have unique perspective, experiences and insight worth exploring, hearing, discovering and knowing.

In my worldwide experience interacting with countless successful and wealthy people throughout Asia and the world, the one thing they all have in common is their humility, cultural sensitivity and sense of humor (being able to not take situations and themselves so seriously). The ability to listen, lighten up and laugh makes them able to connect with anyone, including those unlike themselves and with whom they sometimes may disagree. Hence they are likeable, lovable, and able to work with others; cross barriers, make meaningful connections with people, and collaborate on many profitable and life-changing projects that are of mutual benefit to many constituents. These are simple, profound, critical and foundational secrets to success.

Undoubtedly, these small keys (mostly interpersonal and foundational within their character) continually enable wealthy, savvy and astute individuals to connect with people, transcend conflict and situations to find points of agreement and open big doors to paths of glorious opportunity and limitless profitability.

So as I asked and proposed to my students the following questions, I will now do the same to you my reader. Whether you are Asian or not is irrelevant, because the same questions are insightful, illuminating and pertinent. Though your answers may differ from others, your answers will prove to be insightful and revelatory. In fact your own answers and internal process (reflecting on and answering these questions) will awake you to limiting beliefs, predispositions, cultural presumptions, and erroneous thinking you may have held and adhered to for years regarding yourself (as an Asian or about others of another ethnicity other than yourself).

As someone who has lived and traveled throughout Asia, I have repeatedly seen the thoughts, beliefs and labels given to Chinese by Caucasians in the United States (such as "Chinese are quiet and reserved") to be inaccurate, wrong and misconstrued. Certainly having lived among Chinese and interacted with them daily, I have seen them to be very confident, outspoken, bold, communicative and passionate in their expression (to say the least), and sometimes rather selfish and rude at times (as one of my former middle school

Chinese students in mainland China himself acknowledged when asked to comment on Chinese people and culture). Thus I am not being judgmental, but open and honest (as someone critical of my own race, people and country being the author of "United States of Arrogance").

As a writer, world traveler, and journalist I report what I see, hear, experience, witness and observe. Many times throughout the world in various airports (particularly here in Bangkok), I have seen Chinese in large groups yelling across the room in mass at one another. Thai government officials have even politely asked and gestured to them to calm down and limit the noise on occasions.

It has begun to be comical and fun to watch, as I try to guess what it is they are saying to each other. However when I hear yelling taking place at

5:30am it is a bit early to try to process and evaluate. Therefore I put in my earplugs and seek out a peaceful place to sit hoping my plane arrives on time and gets me out of the noisy terminal where the overwhelming yelling is occurring. This is more true than you know, as I and others have experienced this repeatedly. Yet I wholeheartedly love my Chinese friends throughout the world (as a former Chinese youth Pastor to ABCs - American Born Chinese in Central Florida). I also first taught English as a foreign language in Taipei, Taiwan where I lived next to the national park where the flag was raised daily with a military salute and helicopters sometimes flying in. It was quite an experience.

The two years I spent teaching English in mainland China were divided between Tianjin and

Shenzhen (north and south China respectively). I have no regrets and thoroughly enjoyed the experiences.

The new motion picture "Crazy Rich Asians" inspired the following questions below (asked by various online newspapers mentioned in the resource section) to provoke us all to dig deeper and ask ourselves these primary questions:

1. Who am I?

2. How do I define myself?

3. How do I relate to, label and stereotype others?

Be patient throughout the process and allow your subconscious mind to reveal itself and your rationale mind thereafter to question your snap judgments and any limiting beliefs.

The official video trailer to the film "Crazy Rich Asians" can be seen here:

https://www.youtube.com/watch?v=ZQ-YX-5bAs0

Stars of the film explain why the movie is "groundbreaking" in their opinion:

https://www.youtube.com/watch?v=1G9UNULKI3Q

Using ancient Chinese wisdom and the power of asking thought provoking questions, I am going to exercise restraint and attempt not to play God by voicing my opinions here below. Instead I want to ask the reader to consider and answer the following thought provoking questions.

I can be hired and brought in as a consultant and/or speaker (RevivingNations@yahoo.com) to work with nations, governmental agencies, companies, groups (ethnic, religious or ideological) to provide insight and further guidance. However as I mention here, the initial foundational step is for us all to slow down, pause, and take time to read and examine the questions here below (along with other questions I personalize to your organization, present and propose) to see what we learn about ourselves, our own identity (or organizational identity and assumed national identity), cultural conditioning and how we relate to others (be it correctly, accurately, partially correct/accurate, or incorrectly). Moreover the misnomers, inward untruths, mischaracterized elements and stereotypes about people, miscommunication, misunderstandings, and bad blood that exists between ethnicities, religious and ideological groups; that will sometimes surface through the series of these questions.

As a Life Coach, Wellness Trainer and Worldwide Minister, I travel and speak throughout the world on health, well-being, the power of forgiveness, repentance, reconciliation, team-building, harmony, vision, unification, collaboration and leadership. These exercises and efforts take time, which like the series of questions below will purify hearts to produce higher level thinking, lasting fruit, increased productivity, greater performance, improved productivity and an increase in profitability.

Consider the following questions:

Remember questions open the door to meaningful and transformative conversations, spirited discussions, more deeper high level questions, further examination and exploration, and more transformation. Thus the facilitation and exploration of meaningful questions has more value than one person playing the preacher and trying to put his or her map on you and telling you how to think. Therefore embrace and enjoy the journey of discovery with me.

1.) Does the film "Crazy Rich Asians" truly and fully represents all Asians (or perhaps only rich Chinese)? How so, or how not? Take time to explore your answers and don't be too proud or presumptive to avoid taking the time to do so (as it is when you truly slow down and take time to think and meditate on these matters that illumination and revelation emerge and come forth).

2.) Does the film reinforce the stereotype that Asians are materialistic?

3.) Are Asian Americans truly a 'model minority' others races of people should strive to emulate and be like? Why or why not?

4.) Does the film portray Singapore as being mono-cultural, rather than the multicultural country it truly is? What is valuable or dangerous about such a perception, both within Asia and elsewhere throughout the world?

5.) Is the "crazy rich Asian" wealth gap truly as large as the film purports? Are wealth gaps earned or inherited? Do you believe wealth and opportunities often come to certain Asians because of their race and connections? Why or why not (provide examples).

6.) Does the film simplify Asian geography for viewers or further complicate it? Explain your answer.

7.) What is the back story and origin of the film? What do you know about the history and literature that preceded the making of the film? Did the film stray from the literature and history in any way? What was the original intention of the book?

8.) Is the film a movie or movement? Explain your answer. If the film is in fact a movement leading to something greater, what exactly is that and how shall it be accomplished (and what efforts and actions are further needed to make that movement's dream a living reality)?

9.) What is the "far weightier conversation" that eclipses the million-dollar gems in the film? What aspects about culture, identity, avarice, motives, intermarriage, matchmaking, and relational compatibility touch and speak to you?

10.) How do you feel about the lack of browner faces in the film (considering Singapore has large Malay and Indian populations not represented in the film)?

11.) Do you agree with some on Twitter who nicknamed the film #CrazyRichEastAsians, #CrazyRichMongoloids and #CrazyRichEastLightSkinnedAsians? Why or why not?

12.) Why have Asian actors struggled for decades to gain visibility in the United States film industry?

13.) How do you feel about Asian whitewashing of characters in Hollywood films? What exactly is "whitewashing" and does this assertion have any merit, or are Asians just not willing to admit to themselves Hollywood has preferences when conducting casting for roles. How can "whitewashing" be done away with and Asians be given equal access to acting jobs in Hollywood and elsewhere worldwide?

14.) When a film is made about the rescue of the 12 Thai boys from the Tham Luang cave, would you like to see Caucasian actors play the roles? Why or why not? If white actors are given the roles of Thai boys, what if anything is wrong with this type of casting and filmmaking? Do other nations in Asia make movies patterned after Hollywood, but use only local talent to star in these roles? Is there anything wrong with this? Should Asian nations make their own movies if they want an only Asian cast of stars?

15.) Do Hollywood, Bollywood and movie producers have a moral imperative to cultivate, embrace and showcase diversity when possible to truthfully and adequately represent countries and characters in a culturally sensitive and truthful fashion? Why or why not?

16.) Why are human beings fascinated with extreme wealth? Are humans somehow inspired by watching others "live the good life" on film? If so, how?

17.) How is the film "Crazy Rich Asians" similar and/or different from the 2005 award-winning Memoirs of a Geisha?

18.) How many years has it been since "The Joy Luck Club," the last movie with an all-Asian cast to get a wide release at the movie box office in theaters worldwide? What does that span of time and gap in movie producing tell you about

Hollywood and its attitudes toward Asian

Americans?

19.) Were Asians "clapping, gasping, and crying"

(in your opinion) because the film "Crazy Rich

Asians" was outstanding and unique, or because

they saw themselves on the big screen in movie

theaters and felt they could identify with the

characters?

20.) How well does the film "Crazy Rich Asians"

truly represent you, your family, and Asians you

personally know?

21.) What disparate perceptions do you have about

the film "Crazy Rich Asians"?

22.) Do you believe this film will further open the door for a variety of new stories from Asian filmmakers and actors? What stories and aspects of Asian society would you like to see portrayed in movies? (For example "Slum Dog Millionaire" was a film made in India that showed poverty and opportunity occurring at the same time in society).

23.) What milestones were achieved by "Crazy Rich Asians" worth noting? What future milestones should be pursued?

24.) Beyond Jon Chu's movie, what other films have Constance Wu, Awkwafina, Michelle Yeoh, and Gemma Chan starred and acted in? Who are your favorite Asian actors and are they well known worldwide? If not, what will it take to make nationally known actors world famous? Is fame and fortune important, or are there other aspects of filmmaking worth focusing upon?

Consider the movie business questions below.

25.) Why are Chinese companies buying movie producing companies in America and around the world? What are their intentions and plans?

26.) How can Asians seize opportunities to not only distribute films, but also create them? (Read the SCMP soft power article to help illuminate your thinking and answers.)

27.) How is China remaking the global film industry? (Read the Time article in the resource section.)

28.) How effective are movies at influencing and persuading mindsets of people? Do you see any problem with movies negatively influencing younger and older generations? Why for years have Indian cinemas shown predominately Hindi films and kept out other foreign films (a paradigm that occurs in America also and likely elsewhere worldwide)?

29.) Do you think movies can influence and change cultures, customs and traditions within Asia, America and around the world? If so, how should movies be made to positively impact culture and people? Can films be used as a means of propaganda to control public opinion and manufacture societal consent? If so, is that good or bad for society, citizenry, civil society, freedom of thought, and the future well-being of nations?

30.) How can movies be used to increase global understanding among peoples, cultures and unify us as people? Should movies be made to unify us in thinking, speech and behavior? Or perhaps, should movies be used to widen and deepen our thoughts, while encouraging our own individuality and authenticity so we pursue our unique purpose and discover and give birth to our individual voice?

Sources and Resources:

We Need to Talk About Crazy Rich Asians

https://www.wired.com/story/crazy-rich-asians-conversation/

'It's not a movie, it's a movement': Crazy Rich Asians takes on Hollywood

https://www.theguardian.com/film/2018/aug/11/crazy-rich-asians-movie-kevin-kwan-jon-m-chu-constance-wu

'Crazy Rich Asians' the poster child of diversity? It's only skin-deep

https://www.scmp.com/comment/insight-opinion/united-states/article/2161470/crazy-rich-asians-poster-child-diversity-its

12 Chinese Owned Media Companies, From Dick Clark Productions to AMC

https://www.thewrap.com/hollywood-companies-owned-by-china/

Does China's buying spree of Hollywood studios project soft power? Not so easy

https://www.scmp.com/business/companies/article/2086163/does-chinas-buying-spree-hollywood-studios-project-soft-power-not

China Extends Hollywood Push with $1 Billion Paramount Investment

https://www.reuters.com/article/us-viacom-paramount-china-idUSKBN153335

How China Is Remaking the Global Film Industry

http://time.com/4649913/china-remaking-global-film-industry/

Chinese investors flood into Hollywood

https://www.ft.com/content/2cb93908-2c65-11e6-bf8d-26294ad519fc

Chinese billionaire Wang Jianlin makes aggressive moves in Hollywood

http://www.latimes.com/entertainment/envelope/cotown/la-et-ct-wanda-hollywood-20160928-snap-story.html

The Chinese billionaire trying to take over Hollywood: He's already bought all AMC theaters and the makers of Jurassic World - now wants to pour billions into ALL six major film studios

https://www.dailymail.co.uk/news/article-3899612/Chinese-billionaire-Wang-Jianlin-owns-AMC-theater-chain-wants-Hollywood.html

It's Official: China's Wanda Acquires Legendary
Entertainment for $3.5 Billion

https://www.hollywoodreporter.com/news/official-
chinas-wanda-acquires-legendary-854827

Wanda's purchase of Legendary shows how
Hollywood is moving closer to China

https://qz.com/591988/wandas-purchase-of-
legendary-shows-how-hollywood-is-moving-closer-
to-china/

Tensions flare between US and China, this time
in Hollywood

https://www.cnbc.com/2017/04/20/why-china-
hollywood-deals-have-come-to-a-screeching-
halt.html

China & Hollywood: What Lies Beneath & Ahead
In 2017

https://deadline.com/2017/01/china-hollywood-
deals-2017-donald-trump-1201875991/

China Rising: How Four Giants Are
Revolutionizing the Film Industry

https://variety.com/2015/film/asia/china-rising-
quartet-of-middle-kingdom-conglomerates-
revolutionizing-chinese-film-industry-1201421685/

Chinese conglomerate Dalian Wanda buys Dick Clark productions for $1bn

https://www.theguardian.com/film/2016/nov/03/dalian-wanda-buys-dick-clark-productions-wang-jianlin

"Made In China" Rap Song
Higher Brothers x Famous Dex - Made In China (Prod. Richie Souf)

https://www.youtube.com/watch?v=rILKm-DC06A&index=1&list=RDrILKm-DC06A

U.S. Census Bureau Current World Population

https://www.census.gov/popclock/print.php?component=counter

Diaspora defined

https://www.dictionary.com/browse/diaspora

ASEAN: The Association of Southeast Asian Nations

https://www.cfr.org/backgrounder/asean-association-southeast-asian-nations

The Countries in Asia

https://www.ranker.com/list/the-countries-in-asia/best-world-journeys

List of Asian Countries by Population

https://en.wikipedia.org/wiki/List_of_Asian_countri
es_by_population

Geography of Asia

https://en.wikipedia.org/wiki/Geography_of_Asia

Can China's Economy Thrive with a Censored
Internet?

http://business.time.com/2011/10/26/can-chinas-
economy-thrive-with-a-censored-internet/

China's Internet Censorship Is Influencing Digital
Repression Around The World, Report Warns

http://time.com/5441350/freedom-house-web-
report-2018-china/

Five Ways China Has Become More Repressive
Under President Xi Jinping

http://time.com/4519160/china-xi-jinping-cecc-
human-rights-rule-of-law/

Justice Dept. Backs Suit Accusing Harvard of
Discriminating Against Asian-American Applicants

https://www.nytimes.com/2018/08/30/us/politics/asi
an-students-affirmative-action-harvard.html

Lawsuit accusing Harvard of bias against Asian-Americans heads to trial

https://www.scmp.com/news/world/united-states-canada/article/2166294/does-harvard-discriminate-against-asian-americans

Feds investigate allegations of anti-Asian American discrimination at Yale

https://www.nbcnews.com/news/asian-america/feds-investigate-allegations-anti-asian-american-discrimination-yale-n913566

The Rise and Fall of Affirmative Action

https://www.newyorker.com/magazine/2018/10/15/the-rise-and-fall-of-affirmative-action

Justice Department sides with Asian American students in Harvard bias lawsuit

https://www.theguardian.com/education/2018/aug/30/harvard-university-racism-bias-lawsuit-asian-american-students-justice-department

Justice Department sides with Asian-Americans suing Harvard over admissions policy

https://edition.cnn.com/2018/08/30/politics/harvard-justice-department-affirmative-action-asian-americans-lawsuit/index.html

Does Harvard Treat Asian-American Applicants Unfairly? The Case Goes To Trial

https://www.npr.org/2018/10/15/656974751/does-harvard-treat-asian-american-applicants-unfairly-the-case-goes-to-trial

U.S. Investigating Yale Over Complaint of Bias Against Asian-American Applicants

https://www.nytimes.com/2018/09/26/us/politics/yale-asian-americans-discrimination-investigation.html

Yale is Under Federal Investigation for Alleged Discrimination Against Asian Americans

https://www.forbes.com/sites/susanadams/2018/09/26/yale-is-under-federal-investigation-for-alleged-discrimination-against-asian-americans/#25cb7fd705fd

Yale Says It Too Is Under DOJ Scrutiny for Asian American Bias

https://www.bloomberg.com/news/articles/2018-09-26/yale-says-it-too-is-under-doj-scrutiny-for-asian-american-bias

Feds Investigate Claim of Racial Bias at Yale University

https://www.cbsnews.com/news/feds-justice-department-investigation-discrimination-allegations-yale-university-today-2018-09-26/

After Harvard, Yale is Now Being Investigated for Discriminating Against Asian American Applicants

https://www.scmp.com/news/world/united-states-canada/article/2165898/yale-says-it-target-federal-anti-discrimination

Yale is New Target over Alleged Anti-Asian Bias

https://www.insidehighered.com/admissions/article/2018/09/27/us-reveals-investigation-alleged-anti-asian-bias-yale

Hong Kong - Zhuhai - Macau Bridge

https://www.scmp.com/topics/hong-kong-zhuhai-macau-bridge

World's longest sea crossing is finally finished, but Hong Kong-Zhuhai-Macau bridge has come at a high cost

https://www.scmp.com/news/hong-kong/transport/article/2169199/decade-deaths-and-delays-worlds-longest-sea-crossing

'Ban women drivers': China's sexism surfaces after bus plunges into river

https://www.scmp.com/news/china/society/article/2170766/after-bus-plunges-yangtze-river-chinas-sexism-surfaces

Public transport subsidy for Hong Kong commuters to start from January with government opting to 'keep it simple' and not means tested

https://www.scmp.com/news/hong-kong/transport/article/2171253/hong-kong-commuters-get-bonus-january-next-government

Paul with former United States President

Jimmy Carter and his wife Rosalynn

Paul F. Davis is a University and Career Counselor serving Global Scholars who has worked at Texas A&M International University and for the American China Exchange Society. Paul has earned 4 Master degrees with the highest honors from the University of Texas (Educational Leadership), New York University (Global Affairs), Michigan State College of Law (Global Food Law), the University of Alabama (Health). Paul completed his training in University and Career Counseling with the University of California at Los Angeles.

Paul is a Worldwide Motivational Speaker who has touched 89 nations speaking for the U.S. Military, Companies, Cruise Lines at Sea, Colleges and Universities throughout the globe.

Paul is a Florida and Arizona certified educator,
along with being the author of 50+ books including:
- Update Your Identity
- Integrity of Heart
- Healthy Relationships
- College Match and Self-Discovery
- College Admissions Secrets & Interview
Strategies
- Theater & Arts College Students
- Undocumented Students Strategy to Study in USA
- International Student Engagement Success
Strategies
- Educational Leadership and School Instructional
Improvement
- Charter Schools: Faith, Free Choice and Inferior
Education for Profit Preying on Minorities
- United States of Arrogance
- The Future of Food
- Geostrategy to Protect Environmental Health &
Food Security
- Breakthrough For A Broken Heart
- Empowering & Liberating Women To Achieve
Greatness
- Dating, Relationships, Love and Marriage

Many more books and videos can be seen at Paul's website below. Please also connect with Paul via social media.

www.PaulFDavis.com

www.Linkedin.com/in/worldproperties

www.Facebook.com/speakers4inspiration

www.Twitter.com/PaulFDavis

RevivingNations@yahoo.com

www.ingramcontent.com/pod-product-compliance
Lightning Source LLC
Chambersburg PA
CBHW051417250726
48655CB00003B/1095